Team Building Events & Activities for Managers - T.E.A.M. Series

TEAM
COMMUNICATION ACTIVITIES

Tyler Hayden
TeamBuildingActivities.com

A collection of classic initiative tasks that will help you facilitate experiences that will bring your team together, by taking them outside the box.

ISBN: 978-1-897050-64-4

BUILD YOUR TEAM'S
COMMUNICATION
WITH CLASSIC INITIATIVES

Tyler Hayden

Warning - Use at Your Own Risk

Improper use of the contents described herein may result in serious injury or loss. The activities should not be attempted without the supervision of a trained and properly qualified leader.

Neither the author, publisher, seller or any distributor of this publication assumes any liability for loss or damage, direct or consequential to the reader or others resulting from the use of the materials contained herein, whether such loss or damages results from errors, omissions, ambiguities or inaccuracies in the materials contained herein or otherwise. No warranties, express or implied, as to the merchantability or as to fitness for any particular use or purpose are intended to arise out of the sale or distribution of this publication and this publication is sold "as is" and "with all faults." The liability of the author, publisher, seller, or any distributor of this publication on account of any such errors, omissions, or ambiguities, shall in any event, be limited to the purchase price of this publication.

Copyright © 2017 by Tyler Hayden Inc.
TEAM - Team Building Events & Activities for Manager Series is the property of Tyler Hayden Inc.

All rights reserved. No part of this publication may be reproduced, stored in a retrieval system or transmitted in any form or by any means, electronic, mechanical, photocopying, recording, or otherwise, without the prior written permission of the owner.

Made in Canada.

Communication Activities

www.teambuildingactivities.com/classic

01:55/04:20

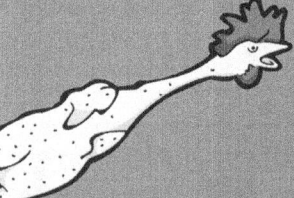

MINE FIELD
WITH TYLER HAYDEN

Communication is a skill that you can learn. It's like riding a bicycle or typing. If you're willing to work at it, you can rapidly improve the quality of every part of your life.

- Brian Tracy

MINE FIELD

Quick Description:

Blindfolded member walks through a zone covered with mouse traps and stuffed toys. This member is being lead by only a trusted voice of another team member. All the while other members of the group try to lead them off course and into "danger."

Time it takes:

30 to 60 minutes

Terminal Objective

The learners will be able to demonstrate and practice skills in communication.

Enabling Objectives

The learners will be able to:

- guide a partner verbally through the task;
- utilize appropriate motivators;
- practice verbal communication techniques;
- apply skills to treatment of others;
- realize varying "tenderness" and cultural differences in others; and
- have fun.

Initiative Task

Mine Field

- sighted partners (guide/leader/supervisor) taking their blindfolded counterpart (learner/employee/student) through a booby trapped field (contact time) of mouse traps (set them for added challenge), eggs, sponges, and human distractions;
- leaders will commit to getting their peers through the program period without springing any of the mines.

Mine field is set up like this:

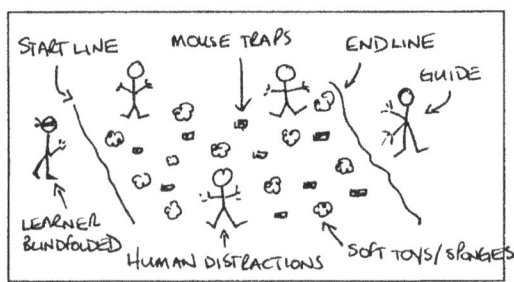

- one pair at a time will have the leader at one end zone, first contact day (i.e. first day on the job/first day of new project, etc), while the group member is at the other, program exit (has experience in the presented project/task and is at the end to provide guidance through the project);
- the spaces indicated above have human distractions placed in them on the field. Their characters are mom or dad, peers, and academics (or relative to your business i.e. project manager, customer, competition, etc.). Remaining people in the group will become silent sidelines with their bumpers up, but after each new team experience, exchange roles;
- communicating only verbally the leader will guide the group member safely through the mine field. If the group member touches a mouse trap or egg (besides potential pain or gooeyness) they will be required to take off their blindfold and return to the beginning as a disgruntled employee/student/etc!;

- the team can start again, but first the leader must say what they did well prior to the group member's unfortunate demise and how they can replicate what they did well for success in the future;
- if the leader wishes, they can lead the group member to pickup sponges which represent good decisions and the group member should identify what one good decision they can make during the activity. (You can take this one step further and have both individuals relate their comments to tangible examples during their future program period.);
- you can increase the challenge by asking group members if they would like to take off their shoes to cross the mine field. This would represent cultural differences as a group member who hasn't been exposed to much or has a different tolerance level could stand to get really hurt. Tell the participants about the group member being very tender and ask them how they are going to need to respond to their needs, prior to their peer crossing the field. This could bring out some interesting debriefing points, but be careful, only add this if you feel your group is ready... so people don't get hurt.

Debrief

This, as always, will depend on the unique experience of each group. However, some of the important questions you might want to ask include:

- What did each thing represent (i.e. egg, mouse trap, distractions, etc.)?
- How did the distractions affect the person going through the maze?
- How can you make it so that you can more effectively communicate with the employee/team member/student?
- What other noises are there in life that make it hard for us to communicate with someone? or them with us?
- What types of nonverbal communications may have helped?
- How did the person picking up the toys have to listen?
- How do you listen to someone giving you direction?
- How do you feel when you pick up a toy as a sender? a receiver?
- What ways can we ensure that we communicate effectively to people?
- If you were communicating effectively what would I see you doing?

WHADYESAY?
WITH TYLER HAYDEN

It takes two to speak the truth - one to speak and another to hear.

- Henry David Thoreau

WHADYESAY?

Intrapersonal Visual/Spatial Mathematical/Logical Verbal/Linguistic

Quick Description:

One team member attempts to get another team member to duplicate a drawing. The trick is only one person gets to see the drawing and must verbally communicate to the other what it looks like so that they can draw it on a piece of paper.

Time it takes:

15 to 25 minutes

Terminal Objective:

In this session team members will expand their knowledge of communicating using the power of multiple intelligences.

Enabling Objectives:

The learners will be able to:

- explore the communication process.
- apply what they know of multiple intelligences to communicating with others.
- express why multiple ways of communicating the same idea are often necessary to reach your cohort of direct reports.

Initiative Task

Whadyesay?

Set Up:
- Photocopy of the "Supervising with Intelligence" for each person.
- Photocopy of the "7 C's of Communication"
- Pens for everyone.
- Blank pieces of paper.
- Photocopy of "Shapes and Such" for the "leader."
- Meeting space.

Activity:
- Invite each person to take the blank piece of paper and turn their chair around so that their back is to you. Next, tell them that you will describe a series of shapes that are on the page in front of you. The team members job is to draw an exact replica of what you are communicating on the page in front of them.
- If the team members have no questions, begin.
- When you are finished compare your selected graphic with theirs.
- Ask the team member, "What worked really well when I was communicating with you? What things did I say or do that helped you to recreate the graphic?" Some answers might include: I asked you clarifying questions, you were exact in what you described, you were patient and waited till I told you I was ready, your voice was clear, you were concise in your directions, etc.
- Now ask the team member, "What are some of the things that you do best when you are communicating with others on your team?"
- Then ask the team member to look at the Supervising with Intelligence graphic and ask, "We know that there are different types of learners on our team. Do those different learns like to be communicated with differently? Then ask, "What specific things could you do differently to get your messaging across to a staff team?"
- General Information on the 7 C's of Communication:

In business communication there is an accepted practice for effective communication called the 7 C's. According to www.mindtools.com they are:

Clear	*Concise*	*Concrete*
Correct	*Coherent*	*Complete*
	Courteous	

- As a leader it is imperative that when you are communicating with your staff regardless of their learning style that you keep the 7 C's in mind. By taking the time to use this tool you will improve your ability to connect (another c - LOL) with the intended recipient of your information.
- **Clear** - Always be sure as to why you are communicating a piece of information. Keep the message transmission as exact as possible in the minimum amount of words. And as always don't leave the recipient of the message struggling to "read between the lines."
- **Concise** - Stick to the point. Don't ramble on or repeat yourself. Be efficient with your messages so that you aren't using up extra sentences or time to get the same point across more simply.
- *Concrete* - You have delivered a content, fact and detail rich message with laser focus. You send a message that can be built on because it is so solid.
- *Correct* - A correct message is not only correct in content, but also delivered in a way that matters to the recipients. Know your audience in the way you speak, what you say, and how you go about delivering it.
- *Coherent* - When your message is delivered in a coherent way it is relevant, well connected to the main topic, delivered logically and in a tone consistent with the topic of the message.
- *Complete* - After you have delivered your message the recipient has enough information to understand the entire message and if necessary take the correct actions.
- *Courteous* - Even the most severe messages should be delivered in a friendly, open and honest way. Keeping the needs of others in mind helps us to ensure that we are being courteous to them.

Debrief:

- Guide the team members, "Pick one message that you have to deliver on a regular basis to your team. Knowing now about the 7 C's and applying Supervising with Intelligence - how can you deliver that same message better?"
- Now role play and have the team member try delivering that message while pretending you are the staff recipient of the message.

Learning Styles of My Team
Supervising with Intelligence

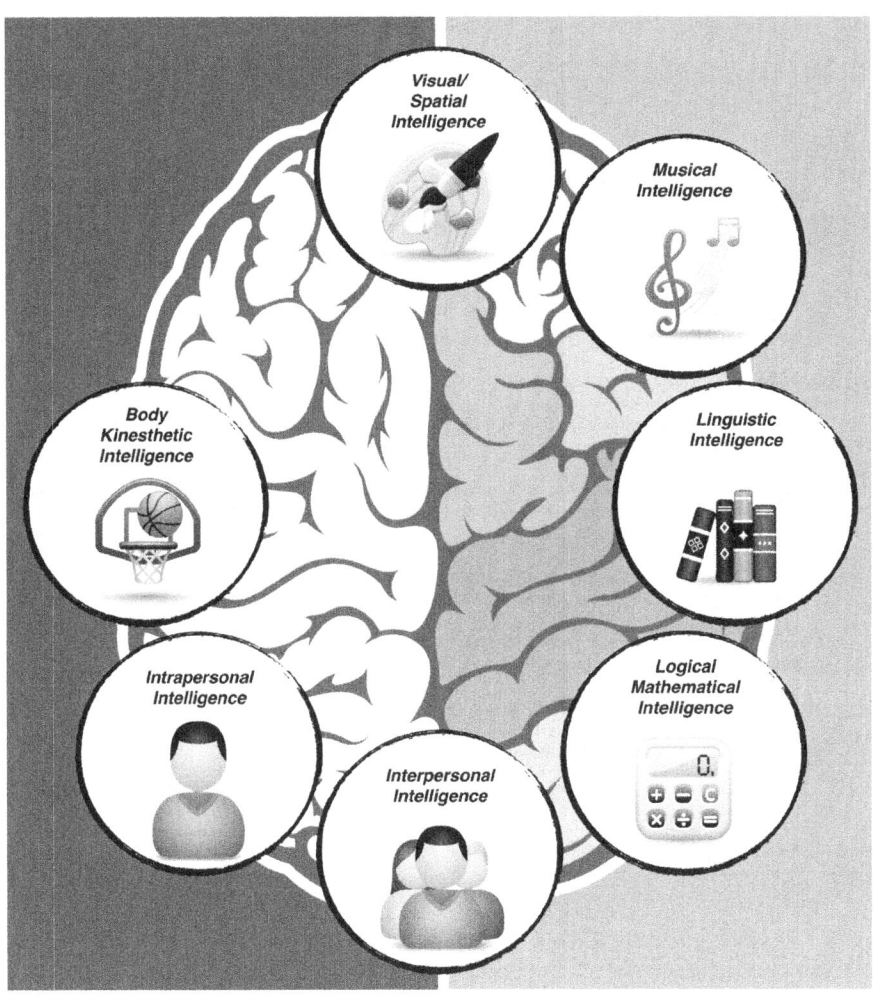

Communicating with Different Styles of People
7 Cs of Communication

7 Cs of Communication

Clear - Always be sure of why you are communicating a piece of information. Keep the message as exact as possible in the minimum amount of words. And as always don't leave the recipient of the message struggling to "read between the lines."

Concise - Don't ramble on or repeat yourself. Be efficient with the words in your messages.

Concrete - You have delivered a content, fact, and detail rich message with laser focus. You send a message that can be built upon because it is so solid.

Correct - A correct message is not only correct in content, but also delivered in a way that matters to the recipients. Know your audience in the way you speak, what you say, and how you go about delivering your message.

Coherent - When your message is delivered in a coherent way it is relevant to the main topic, delivered logically and in a tone consistent with the topic of the message.

Complete - After you have delivered your message the recipient has enough information to understand the entire message and, if necessary, take the correct actions.

Courteous - Even the most severe messages should be delivered in a respectful, open, and honest way. Keeping the needs of others in mind helps us to ensure we are being courteous to them.

Tyler Hayden Inc. ©, www.mindtools.com

Communicating with Different Styles of People
Shapes and Such

Instructions: Guide your partner to draw one of the 4 pictures on the sheet below. Your partner will have their back to you while you describe how to draw the picture. The goal is for your partner to recreate on their blank page the box you have on your page.

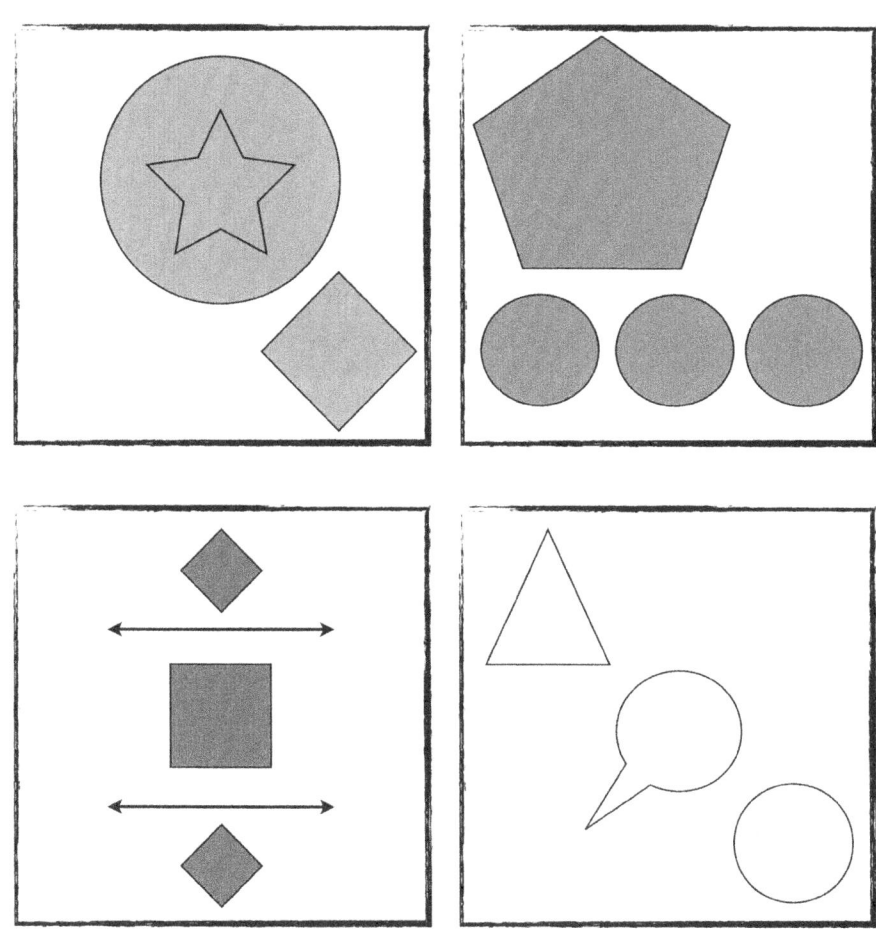

Tyler Hayden Inc. ©

www.teambuildingactivities.com/classic

01:55/04:20   720

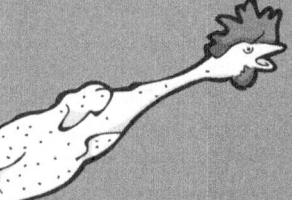

SCARECROW
WITH TYLER HAYDEN

Communication is about often hearing what isn't being said.

- Tyler Hayden

SCARECROW

Quick Description:

A blindfolded group builds a scarecrow out of provided supplies. Then once complete they accessorize the scarecrow with items that metaphor skills which a good communicator demonstrates.

Time it takes:

40 to 70 minutes

Terminal Objective

The learners will be able to discover skills that will improve their ability to communicate with others.

Enabling Objectives

Learners will be able to:

- talk about one specific communication skill that each learner used effectively;
- practice communicating with their colleagues;
- be involved in a task that stretches learners' current communication skills;
- practice non-verbal communication skills;
- practice verbal communication skills; and
- have fun.

Initiative Task

Scarecrow

This session is designed to provide your learners with new communication skills. Spend about 5 minutes discussing how being an effective communicator enables learners to do their job more effectively and efficiently. Ask first, "What is communication? When do we do it? and How?" Then, have each learner verbally finish the following open ended statement: "When I am an effective communicator you see me..."

- have the group sit in a circle invite learners to put on blindfolds;
- ask learners to listen carefully so that they understand all the directions because you are only saying them once, as listening is of equal importance in the communication loop as presenting the information;
- explain to learners their task as you pass out one of the following items to each person: a hay bale (or fabric scraps), a long sleeve shirt, pants, a hat, boots, a chair, a belt, cordage, work gloves, safety scissors, and a small burlap bag.
- challenge the learners to build a scarecrow using the materials provided. Tell them that they have 15 minutes to complete the task (but who's kidding who? How are they gonna keep time 'cause they can't see anyway? So it can go longer or shorter depending on their efficiency and effectiveness... you are in charge.);
- when learners have completed the task have them remove their blindfolds and celebrate their successful construction of a scarecrow; and
- if it doesn't seem like they're doing so well have 'em take off their blindfolds and complete the task sighted.
- following the building of the scarecrow you can have your learners accessorize the scarecrow and make "tags" and stick the accessory. The accessories are metaphors for attributes of a great team communicator (i.e. sunglasses = cool under pressure, or fancy shoes = expresses professionalism).
- You will set this up by providing learners with cue cards to write their "tag" and tape to stick it to the scarecrow. Then challenge learners to choose an accessory they have with them and a metaphor for communication. It can be set up by asking the following: "Think of an attribute that could be a metaphor that relates to an accessory that you currently have with you (i.e. sunglasses = cool under pressure, reading glasses = can focus on the fine details, etc.). Once you figure out your metaphor, place our item and your "tag" on the scarecrow." Then, have each learner share their tag and item.

Debrief

This, as always, will depend on the unique experience of each group. However, some of the important questions you might want to ask include:

- How did wearing a blindfold force you to communicate?
- Who was communicating well?
- What specifically were those people doing that made them effective communicators?
- When did you communicate well non-verbally? How? Why? With whom?
- When did you communicate well verbally? How? Why? With whom?
- When did you listen well? Why? How were people communicating that encouraged you to listen that way?
- How do you know when others have received what you communicated effectively?
- When are good communication skills important?
- Where does planning come into play for good communication of activities and projects?
- What are 3 ways to effectively communicate an upcoming project?
- Name a way that you have creatively communicated an upcoming event.
- How do you communicate differently with staff? Customers? Executive? Etc.
- How did people encourage feedback from the group?

Team Building Events & Activities for Managers - T.E.A.M. Series

TEAM
LEADERSHIP ACTIVITIES

Tyler Hayden
TeamBuildingActivities.com

A collection of classic initiative tasks that will help you facilitate experiences that will bring your team together, by taking them outside the box.

BUILD YOUR TEAM'S
LEADERSHIP SKILLS
WITH CLASSIC INITIATIVES

Tyler Hayden

Warning - Use at Your Own Risk

Improper use of the contents described herein may result in serious injury or loss. The activities should not be attempted without the supervision of a trained and properly qualified leader.

Neither the author, publisher, seller or any distributor of this publication assumes any liability for loss or damage, direct or consequential to the reader or others resulting from the use of the materials contained herein, whether such loss or damages results from errors, omissions, ambiguities or inaccuracies in the materials contained herein or otherwise. No warranties, express or implied, as to the merchantability or as to fitness for any particular use or purpose are intended to arise out of the sale or distribution of this publication and this publication is sold "as is" and "with all faults." The liability of the author, publisher, seller, or any distributor of this publication on account of any such errors, omissions, or ambiguities, shall in any event, be limited to the purchase price of this publication.

Copyright © 2016 by Tyler Hayden Inc.
Livin' Life Large™ is the property of Tyler Hayden Inc.

All rights reserved. No part of this publication may be reproduced, stored in a retrieval system or transmitted in any form or by any means, electronic, mechanical, photocopying, recording, or otherwise, without the prior written permission of the owner.

Made in Canada.

Leadership Activities

www.teambuildingactivities.com/classic

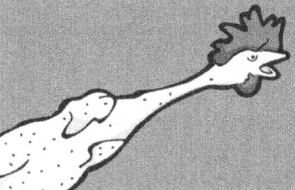

NUCLEAR REACTOR
WITH TYLER HAYDEN

Team building is what you do with people, not to people.

- Tyler Hayden

NUCLEAR REACTOR

Visual/Spatial   Interpersonal   Body/Kinesthetic   Mathematical/Logical

Quick Description:

Members attempt to rebuild a structure of cups and a tennis ball with different constraints of time and relationship. The constraints develop an atmosphere whereby the importance of situational leadership comes to the surface in order to complete the task.

Time it takes:

30 to 45 minutes

Terminal Objective

Learners will investigate the concept of situational leadership through concrete experience with an activity that requires different styles leadership as the situation changes.

Enabling Objectives

The learners will be able to:

- utilize different styles of leadership;
- demonstrate leadership and "followership" roles;
- apply situational leadership to their role as leader;
- observe the effects of different situational leadership roles;
- have fun.

Initiative Task

Nuclear Reactor

- cut your kite string into lengths of about four meters, cutting enough for one per learner;
- tie the strings to the rubber band at equal intervals, kind of like spokes on a wagon wheel;
- place the two cups together in the center of the teaching space (on floor or table) with a tennis ball inside the one cup;
- lay the rubber band and strings down beside the cups and tennis ball with the strings radiating out, just like that wagon wheel;
- the room should be dimly lit (a black light makes things look really cool). You should now have set up the nuclear reactor (cups), radioactive material (tennis ball), and clean up equipment (rubber band and strings).

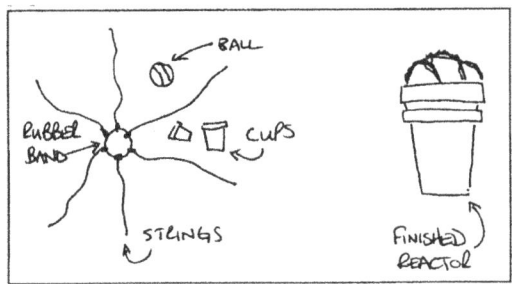

Sample Presentation:

- You meet the learners outside the reactor room, and in a refined and distinguished voice you say, "Hello, and welcome to Homer Simpson's Nuclear Power Generation & Donuts. I would like to thank you for coming to view the facility. You know, it's not everyday we get nuclear technicians of your caliber to our site... (nervously). Well that's not to mean that we skimp on safety standards, of course. (calm again) Please come with me and we'll tour the site. Inside this room is our pride and joy - Spooo (ooops spelled backwards), one of our best reactors, which we are currently unveiling."

- "You'll notice that we have a state of the art reinforced nuclear reactor, whose walls are like those that surround every building at our company. Next is the radioactive material. This powerful stuff is the project we are working on. And last, but certainly not least, is this nuclear crane. It's the device we use to build nuclear power generators. Much like how team members build their portion of a good project. Each extending handle is an individual member of your work team. Now if you would just step this way we'll go to the lunch room for afternoon tea, shall we."
- Then just as you are leaving the area around the power generator you conveniently trip and spill the nuclear reactor emptying the contents and generally busting the reactor apart. When your boss finds out you're in trouble. Just then, as part of the risk management plan for the generating station, the double plated steel doors bolt and lock. A voice (really you using a different voice - lol) pipes up, "The system has experienced failure in the main Spooo generator. All personnel except for rescue crews are to leave the building immediately. Total containment of the source is required in three minutes. Rescue crews need to utilize the crane in order to reconstruct the reactor as it stood before."
- If the group doesn't catch on to the fact that they are the only ones who can save the world from another nuclear disaster then you should come out of your shock state and say, "It's up to you to use the crane to contain the radioactive material."
- give the team only 3 minutes to complete the task, and keep the pressure on by letting them know how long they have left i.e. 3 minutes remaining, 2 minutes remaining, etc., etc.

Debrief

The activity is designed to a create situation where a task oriented leader is required to effectively resolve it during its first take. While other issues may arise, please try to stay focused on situational leadership - particularly task leadership, its outcomes, its benefits, and ways and whens to do it in the life of a project. Included at the end of this session write up is a brief discussion about situational leadership which will help with your debrief.

- How does time pressure necessitate a different style of leadership?

- What did you do effectively to get the job done?
- What were peoples roles within the task? What was required for each of the roles? What's the difference between leadership and followership? Why are both required in a time pressured situation like this?
- How did you decide who would lead? Was there time for collaboration and the democratic process?
- When in the life of a project would a leader need to lead this way? Why?
- What are the shortcomings of this style of leadership? What are the benefits? What should a leader do at the end of using this style to ensure engagement with the team?

Activity Take 2

- now, give the group as long as they need to get the structure back together;
- by eliminating the time constraints the group will most likely alter the way in which they interact, moving into participating and delegating quadrants. Let them go until they achieve success or extreme frustration (if the latter occurs and the group consents you can offer to revisit it later);
- remember it's not the product but the process that's important to the debrief so focus on the maintenance behaviors exhibited (talk about the success that the group achieved and let them celebrate it).

Debrief #2

This generation of the activity will create opportunities to exhibit maintenance behaviors. Spend some time debriefing how a maintenance leader will act, the outcomes of these behaviors, benefits, and ways and whens to do it.

- What is the difference in team functioning when the leader has the time to collaborate, and maintain relationships amongst the team?
- How do you feel about the outcome when you get to be part of the solution building? How is that different from more task related situations?
- When is this style of leadership appropriate in the life of a project? How do peoples professional competencies play into this style of leadership?

Situational Leadership
Right Timing Your Leadership

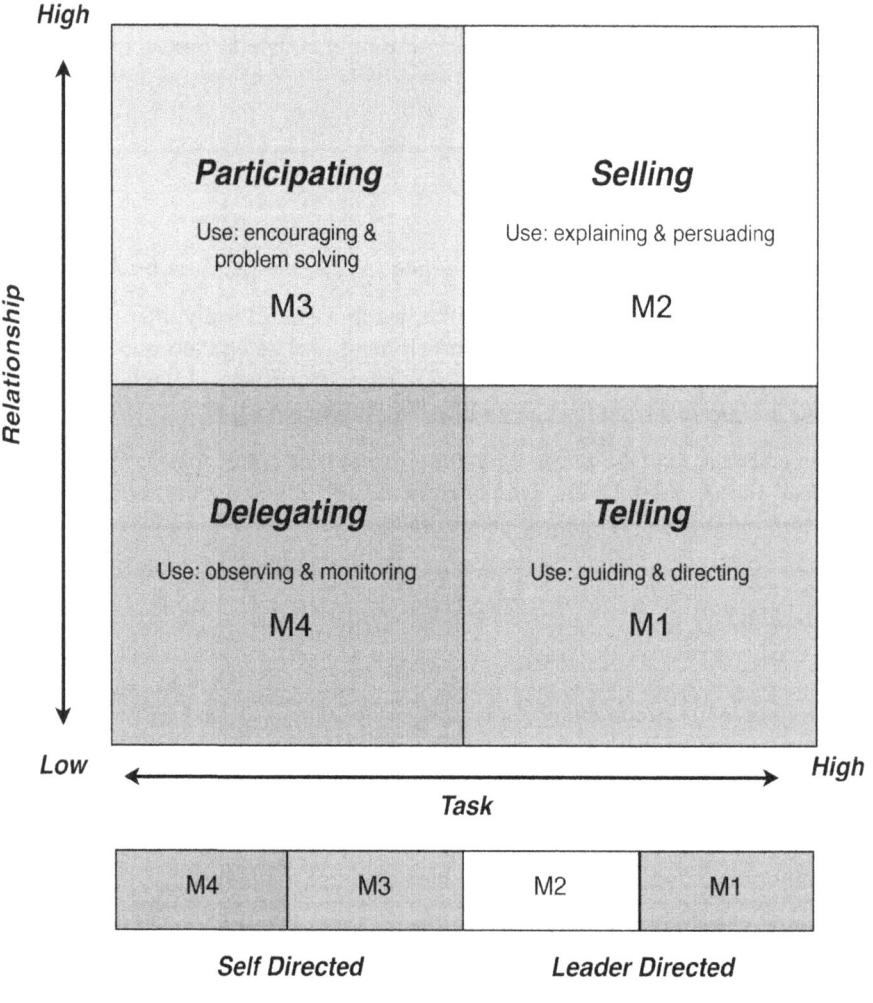

Hersey & Blanchard's Model of Situational Leadership

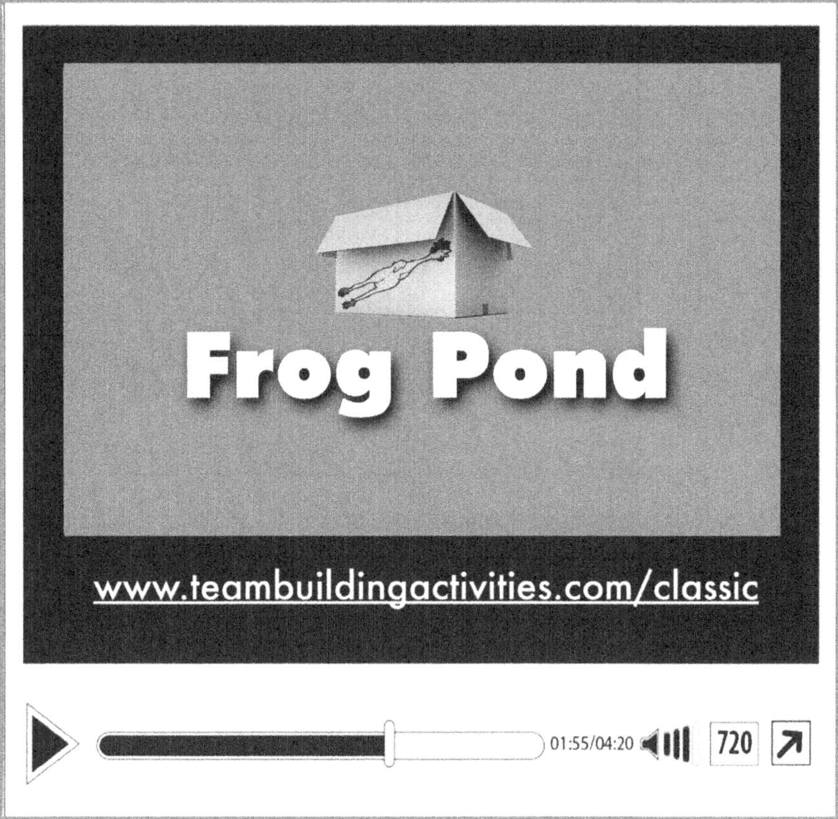

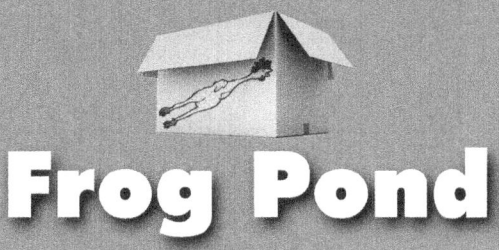

Frog Pond
www.teambuildingactivities.com/classic
01:55/04:20
720

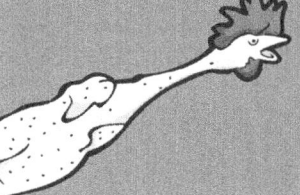

FROG POND

WITH TYLER HAYDEN

Team building is what you do with people, not to people.

- Tyler Hayden

FROG POND

 Visual/Spatial
 Naturalistic
 Body/Kinesthetic
 Interpersonal

Quick Description:

Half your team (frogs) attempt to cross a defined area (pond) while the other half of your team (rascals) throws stuffed toys (rocks) at the frogs. Each half of the team must work collaboratively to realize their objectives (hitting frogs or getting safely to the other side).

Time it takes:

30 to 45 minutes

Terminal Objective

Learners will investigate the concepts of leadership and collaboration through a concrete experience with its functions and effects on a project.

Enabling Objectives

The participants will be able to:

- explore personal leadership;
- explore the benefits of collaboration;
- complete a task that requires both leadership and collaboration;
- apply leadership and collaboration to their roles within their work team; and
- have fun.

Initiative Task

Frog Pond

Set Up:

- build a playing field that is 15 meters by 5 meters;
- gather up a whole bunch of soft toys;
- you also need enough stepping stones for half your group minus one (or for added challenge two) i.e. 20 participants you need 9 or 8 stepping stones;
- divide your group in half (one half are frogs, the other half, dirty mean little rascals); and
- switch roles so that frogs can be dirty mean little rascals and vice versa.

Rules:

- frogs start at one side of the frog pond and using the lilly pads (stepping stones) to travel across the pond to the other side;
- dirty mean little rascals will throw stones (soft toys) at the traversing frogs trying to hit them, from the waist down, when they are not on the lilly pads;
- frogs are only safe when they are touching the lilly pads or behind either the start or finish line;
- all the frogs must move collectively from the start to the finish;
- dirty mean little rascals can travel up and down the sides of the pond (15 meter side) to gain aim at throwing the *stones* at the frogs;
- if a frog gets hit with a stone the group must go back to the beginning; and
- any other rules that you deem appropriate.

Metaphorm:

- "stones" represent those things that can cause your work team to have alternative success (i.e. lack of communication, lack of planning, lack of financial resources, polarization of the group, etc.)
- "dirty mean little rascals" represent those group members or external naysayers who present behaviors that could cause your group to not achieve success (i.e. blockers, self confessors, sabotagers, etc.);
- "frogs" represent your intact work team (i.e. project team, office team, etc.);
- "frog pond" represents your place of work for your work team (i.e. virtual, office, etc.). And the start finish represent the scope of time allotted for this project.

Debrief

Here are some questions that may help guide your debrief towards the concept of collaborative leadership:

- What did the frogs represent? The dirty mean little rascals? The lilly pads? The frog pond?
- What did the frogs and dirty mean little rascals do prior to the frogs taking the first step across the pond?
- How did the frogs work together to achieve success?
- Why was it important for each frog to work equally to achieve the success of crossing the pond?
- Who was the leader? Were they always the leader? Did anyone else lead at any time?
- What special skills did each frog bring to the task of crossing the pond?
- How do special skills help a group achieve success?
- How do people feel, when a collaborative group works well, about the finished product or service?
- Why do you suppose people feel more empowered about what they have done?

- What becomes the prime motivator behind a collaborative group of leaders?
- When a group of people work together with their special skills we call it collaboration. Knowing that, what is collaborative leadership and how did you just do it?
- What are the benefits of collaborative leadership?
- Groups like the Clinton Administration, PARC (who developed the first personal computer), Apple Computer (who made that computer marketable) all used collaborative groups to achieve success. What does your group need to know about itself in order to collaborate well?
- What do you need to do before you actually start working together as a group in order to create a space in which it is okay to collaborate leadership?
- What one thing can you do that will empower people to get involved in the collaboration within your projects?

Team Building Events & Activities for Managers - T.E.A.M. Series

TEAM
PLANNING ACTIVITIES

Tyler Hayden
TeamBuildingActivities.com

A collection of classic initiative tasks that will help you facilitate experiences that will bring your team together, by taking them outside the box.

BUILD YOUR TEAM'S
PLANNING SKILLS
WITH CLASSIC INITIATIVES

Tyler Hayden

Warning - Use at Your Own Risk

Improper use of the contents described herein may result in serious injury or loss. The activities should not be attempted without the supervision of a trained and properly qualified leader.

Neither the author, publisher, seller or any distributor of this publication assumes any liability for loss or damage, direct or consequential to the reader or others resulting from the use of the materials contained herein, whether such loss or damages results from errors, omissions, ambiguities or inaccuracies in the materials contained herein or otherwise. No warranties, express or implied, as to the merchantability or as to fitness for any particular use or purpose are intended to arise out of the sale or distribution of this publication and this publication is sold "as is" and "with all faults." The liability of the author, publisher, seller, or any distributor of this publication on account of any such errors, omissions, or ambiguities, shall in any event, be limited to the purchase price of this publication.

Copyright © 2016 by Tyler Hayden Inc.
Livin' Life Large™ is the property of Tyler Hayden Inc.

All rights reserved. No part of this publication may be reproduced, stored in a retrieval system or transmitted in any form or by any means, electronic, mechanical, photocopying, recording, or otherwise, without the prior written permission of the owner.

Made in Canada.

Planning Activities

Puzzled Yet?

www.teambuildingactivities.com/classic

PUZZLED YET?
WITH TYLER HAYDEN

Team building is what you do with people, not to people.

- Tyler Hayden

PUZZLED YET?

Interpersonal · **Visual/Spatial** · **Mathematical/Logical** · **Musical**

Quick Description:

Members of your team will explore the importance of project planning by first developing a metaphor for planning and golf. Then, together they will perform a project build and attempt to assemble a puzzle. Links will be explored around puzzle attributes and how they will perform as an effective team member in the planning process.

Time it takes:

40 to 60 minutes

Terminal Objective

Learners will experience a program that exposes them to skills that will enable them to become more effective planners.

Enabling Objectives

Learners will be able to:

- create a mission statement for this intact work team;
- explore how to manage resources (i.e. time, money, people, etc.) effectively to reach their mission;
- maintain dialogue about how to integrate good planning into their experiences as leaders for both self and others;
- perform evaluation strategies both formatively and summatively;
- explore the value in planning for success;
- define the methodology that they utilized to achieve planned successes; and
- have fun.

Initiative Task

Golf Dialogue

- it has been said that golf is the best metaphor for life (actually, by Tiger Woods);
- find out briefly who has played, how you play, etc. Then ask your group to list some of the things at a golf course;
- some of the elements of golfing are: sand and water traps, club houses, paths, golf carts, putting greens, different size clubs, team members, competitors, spectators, parking lots, care takers, sprinkler systems, advertising, managers, grass, trees, animals, etc.;
- start a dialogue with your group on how the game of golf has direct connections to life, for example, the first hole could be getting the scope of work documentation. The second hole could represent getting the team together, the third a significant benchmark, etc., you get the idea... Don't forget sand traps (financial issues), caretakers (ad hoc teams maybe), etc. The first 17 holes could represent milestones that they need to do in the upcoming year to complete the project (the groups mission) an at the end of the course (18th hole) is end of the project. Then they can start a new golf course... filled with new goals; and
- think about some of the above attributes and how they are metaphorically like life, and let your group briefly draw some of the other connections, but focus the majority of your dialogue around missions and goals.

Puzzled Yet!

- have the group sit velcro knees or around a table side-by-side;
- offer them a new challenge as you point to a puzzle box placed out of reach of the learners (preferably in another room);
- the puzzle represents their project... each piece represents an action taken in achieving that mission and when it is effectively attached to another piece you begin to connect actions and build success in an area of the project (i.e. flowers on the puzzle could represent staffing, and the barn the software design)... 20 minutes represents the project lifespan....
- collectively the group must put together the puzzle that is in the box and they only have 20 contact minutes to do so. (This means that the clock starts when anyone is actively working on the puzzle... so if no one is touching the puzzle

- the clock stops... when people are touching the puzzle again the clock starts... pretty simple eh?). This allows them to stop and **revaluate** (an important part of planning), *readjust and resume;*
- ask the group if they have any questions, then invite them to start; and
- have fun and remember to celebrate a job well done! What I do is ask the group to stop at the 20 minutes. Celebrate what they achieved. And let them know that it's the process of planning the puzzle build that matters not the completion of the 1000 pieces.

Debrief

Have your group spend the remaining time talking about what they did that enabled them to create positive outcomes. Some questions you might want to ask include:

- What process did they go through when they were planning to build the puzzle? (Provide follow up questions like: Why did you do the outside pieces first? Why was organizing things in to areas of the puzzle (barn/flowers) important? How was that process like what we need to do for our project plan?)
- How did they allocate resources so that the job was completed efficiently and effectively?
- Have the group write down the process they went through (i.e. mission, planning, division of tasks, revaluation (formative and summative) completion, readjust, resume and celebration.)
- Apply it to project life with questions like: What are the most successful projects you have completed? How did you plan for them? How did the team function within that project plan?
- How do you best use your resources so that you are effectively reaching towards completing your objectives?
- How do you make sure that the job is getting done?
- What can you do to stay excited about each component of the project (objectives) that makes up your picture (mission)?
- What do you do when each piece has been placed to define closure?
- Why is celebration important? How will we celebrate during the project and at the end?

Bannuka

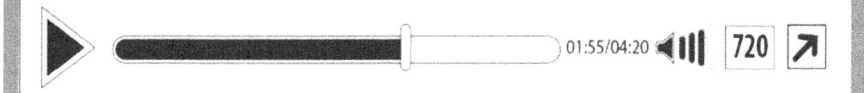

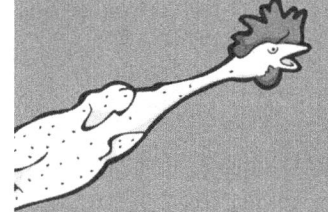

www.teambuildingactivities.com/classic

BANNUKA
WITH TYLER HAYDEN

Team building is what you do with people, not to people.

- Tyler Hayden

BANNUKA

- Visual/Spatial
- Interpersonal
- Body/Kinesthetic
- Mathematical/Logical

Quick Description:

Team members work in small teams to build a "box" to hold their toy car. They must allocate resources and trade for supplies to build their carrier. Teams explore project planning and allocation of resources to complete the task at hand.

Time it takes:

40 to 60 minutes

Terminal Objective

Learners will experience a program that exposes them to skills that will enable them to become more effective planners.

Enabling Objectives

Learners will be able to:

- create a mission for this intact work team;
- explore how to manage resources (i.e. time, money, people, etc.) effectively to reach their mission;
- maintain dialogue about how to integrate good planning into their project and leadership experience;
- perform an evaluation both formatively and summatively; and
- have fun.

Initiative Task

Bunnuka

- have the group sit velcro knees;
- welcome them to Bunnuka the ancient Nova Scotian art of trading - (if you like, spin a yarn about where it originated, why it exists, who designed it, and whatever else you choose... storytelling is fun and adds a bit of humor to the activity - be creative);
- place the following list of supplies on a desk with the corresponding "prices" written on slips of paper;
- the learners' task is to design and build a carrying case large enough to fit their toy car - or whatever else you want, i.e. team memory box, teddy bear to donate to charity, etc. (We often do this this as part of our team building event based on the scouts "Pinewood Derby" - so the box carries and displays the car);
- give the learners a bag of M&M's and tell them that this is will be their currency for this activity and that the building materials are priced in M&M units (i.e. 30 popsicle sticks = 40 M&M's) inform the learners that for every 5 minutes after they have finished their first 5 minutes of planning you will be charging them 5 M&M's (labor charges) and will collect them at the 5, 10, 15, 20, etc. minutes marks. Finally, tell them that they are not allowed to use any supplies other than those on the table in order to build their carrying case;
- ask if anyone has any questions about the project or their task at hand so far;
- their first task is to design a working mission for the project. It will be your job to help facilitate this process so that they hit all the points within a good mission statement. Remember a good mission statement should be written down in less than 100 words and answer the following three questions: 1) What function will you perform as a group?; 2) For whom do you perform this function?; and 3) How do you go about performing this function? (i.e. The Honey Suckers is an efficient and effective planning and development group who is able to build appropriate parking structures for soap box racers in a timely manner to meet external and internal expectations and requirements.);
- once the group has their mission statement they need to talk about how to build their garage and come up with a plan so that the project costs them the least amount of M&M's (because whatever M&M's that they have left over they get

- to eat) - remember to charge them after their first 5 minutes of planning for every five minutes of planning;
- O.K 'nuff said... now it's your group's turn to go unless they have any questions. For your reference the following is the list of supplies and costs:

30 popsicle sticks	-	40 M&M's
Cup of Glue	-	15 M&M's
Leasing Markers	-	10 M&M's per 10 minutes
8.5 x11 Cardboard	-	50 M&M's
3 sheets of Construction Paper	-	10 M&M's
Small Cardboard Box	-	25 M&M's
Labor	-	5 M&M's per 5 minutes
Scissors	-	5 M&M's per 10 minutes
... anything else your choice!		(i.e. yarn, rope, sparkles, etc.)

- have fun and remember to celebrate a job well done!

Debriefing

Have your group spend the remaining time talking about what they did to make this an effective project. Some questions you might want to ask include:

- What process did they go through when they were planning to build this garage structure?
- How did they allocate resources so that the job was completed efficiently and effectively?
- Have the group write down the process they went through (i.e. mission, planning, division of tasks, purchase of supplies, time management, construction, decoration, completion, and celebration.)
- How did they know what the structure should look like (bench marking off of other similar structures that they have seen)?

- Then apply the exercise to their project life by asking questions like, what are the most successful projects you have been involved in? What made them effective?
- What would you do to build a similar garage, only better?
- How do you make sure at the beginning of the project that you will have an effective plan?
- How do you best use your resources to be effective?
- How do you decide who does what?
- How do you make sure that the job is getting done?
- What can you do to keep people excited about their project?
- What do you do when the project is finished to define closure?
- Why is celebration important?

Team Building Events & Activities for Managers - T.E.A.M. Series

TEAM
PROBLEM SOLVING ACTIVITIES

Tyler Hayden
TeamBuildingActivities.com

A collection of classic initiative tasks that will help you facilitate experiences that will bring your team together, by taking them outside the box.

BUILD YOUR TEAM'S
PROBLEM SOLVING
WITH CLASSIC INITIATIVES

Tyler Hayden

Warning - Use at Your Own Risk

Improper use of the contents described herein may result in serious injury or loss. The activities should not be attempted without the supervision of a trained and properly qualified leader.

Neither the author, publisher, seller or any distributor of this publication assumes any liability for loss or damage, direct or consequential to the reader or others resulting from the use of the materials contained herein, whether such loss or damages results from errors, omissions, ambiguities or inaccuracies in the materials contained herein or otherwise. No warranties, express or implied, as to the merchantability or as to fitness for any particular use or purpose are intended to arise out of the sale or distribution of this publication and this publication is sold "as is" and "with all faults." The liability of the author, publisher, seller, or any distributor of this publication on account of any such errors, omissions, or ambiguities, shall in any event, be limited to the purchase price of this publication.

Copyright © 2016 by Tyler Hayden Inc.
Livin' Life Large™ is the property of Tyler Hayden Inc.

All rights reserved. No part of this publication may be reproduced, stored in a retrieval system or transmitted in any form or by any means, electronic, mechanical, photocopying, recording, or otherwise, without the prior written permission of the owner.

Made in Canada.

WWW.TEAMBUILDINGACTIVITIES.COM

Problem Solving

Knot Fun

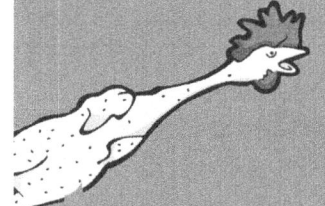

www.teambuildingactivities.com/classic

01:55/04:20 720

KNOT FUN
WITH TYLER HAYDEN

Team building is what you do with people, not to people.

- Tyler Hayden

KNOT FUN

Visual/Spatial · **Interpersonal** · **Body/Kinesthetic** · **Mathematical/Logical**

Quick Description:

The team is presented a rope with knots in it. They will then "stick" their hands to a certain spot in between two of the knots and without anyone removing their hands untie the rope. The problem is resolved when all knots are untied, and no one has let go of the rope.

Time it takes:

40 to 90 minutes (really depends on the group :)

Terminal Objective

The session will provide learners with an opportunity to experience the interpersonal resources that are required for successful issue resolution.

Enabling Objective

The learners will be able to:

- identify the need to ask for help from others;
- discuss how to maximize the resources of the people around you;
- create an opportunity to aid each other in resolving an issue;
- discuss the benefits of helping someone achieve success in issue resolution;
- create a methodology to resolve issues;
- achieve success in resolving an issue; and
- have fun.

Initiative Task

Knot Fun

- the object of this initiative is to have the group undo the knots that are tied in the rope without letting go of the rope (or using their second hand for added challenge).

Briefing

- explain to the group that one of the most important functions they will provide will be that of resolving issues (a.k.a. problem solving- it's semantics for me to make the focus of the session sound as positive as possible); and
- you can either have them share a short issue that they have had to resolve or you can present a major issue that you solved while working in a similar position.

Set Up Considerations

- take a length of rope that measures approximately a meter long for every 3 or 4 people;
- tie overhand knots in the rope at regular intervals. Make enough so that when each member of the group holds onto the rope (with one hand) they have a knot on the left and one on the right of their hand (except for the people on the ends where they will only have a knot on the inside portion of the rope);
- ask the group to pick up the rope with one hand (using whatever hand is most comfortable to them) in between the knots. It looks like this:

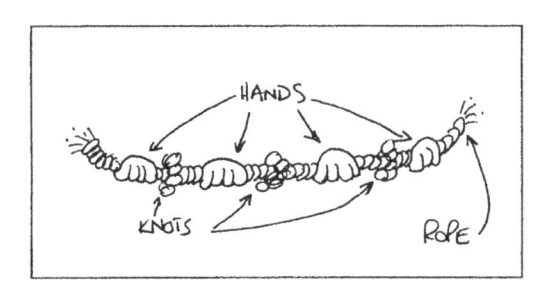

-

- when the members are holding the rope, tell them that their hands are stuck fast to the rope and cannot be moved; now without removing their hands the group must untie the knots in the rope (if they are really fast achieving this, get them to tie a knot into the center of the rope!).

Metaphorm

- resolving issues takes practice and awareness of many external factors;
- in this initiative the "rope" represents a program or responsibility that each person is involved in (project financing, office administration, community development committee, etc.);
- "knots" represent the issues that the group encounters in striving to create a strong project (a knot in a rope reduces the tensile strength considerably!); and
- they "can't let go of the rope" because all members have committed to the project's effective completion.

Debrief

- What do you think the rope represents? the knots? holding on?
- What was the first thing that you did as a group in order to decide how to best untie the knots?
- Tell me all the things that you knew about the rope and the knots from past experiences and your current positions.
- What role did you play in untying the knots? Why did people play different roles in solution building?
- How did you untie the first knot? By untying the first knot what were you able to learn about untying knots? How did you use what you learned?
- How do you apply untying knots to the collective projects that you need to do?
- What things do you now understand about resolving issues (i.e. how do you check your emotions, physically do things, treat others in the group, etc.)?
- What were the specific things you did to solve the issue and in what order did you do them?
- What type of generalizations about issue resolution can you make using the specifics you just identified?
- Name three things you need to do in order to resolve issues as a team.

Punctured Drum

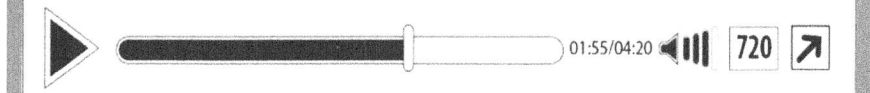

www.teambuildingactivities.com/classic

01:55/04:20   720

PUNCTURED DRUM
WITH TYLER HAYDEN

Team building is what you do with people, not to people.

- Tyler Hayden

PUNCTURED DRUM

- Naturalistic
- Interpersonal
- Body/Kinesthetic
- Mathematical/Logical

Quick Description:

Group members must fill a large bucket littered with holes with water using two smaller buckets. The water must overflow the larger bucket with holes. Teams will use all their resources to plug the holes to ensure that the issue can be resolved.

Time it takes:

40 to 60 minutes

Terminal Objective

The session will provide learners with an opportunity to experience the resources that are required for successful issue resolution.

Enabling Objective

The learners will be able to:

- identify the need to ask for help from others;
- discuss how to maximize the resources of the people around you;
- create an opportunity to aid each other in resolving an issue;
- discuss the benefits of helping someone achieve success in issue resolution;
- create a methodology to resolve issues;
- achieve success in resolving an issue; and
- have fun.

Initiative Task

Punctured Drum

Briefing

- explain to the group that one of the most important functions they will provide will be that of resolving issues (a.k.a. problem solving- it's semantics for me to make the focus of the session sound as positive as possible); and

- you can either have them share a short issue that they have had to resolve or you can present a major issue that you solved while working in a similar position.

Punctured Drum

- the object of this initiative is to have the group overflow the drum (which resembles Swiss cheese). The group is given two buckets to transport the water from the nearby water source to the drum. Only pieces of the learners anatomies may be used to plug the holes.

- the initiative should be set up something like this:

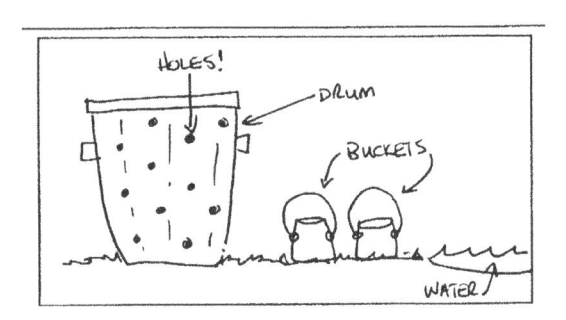

Set Up Considerations:

- place drum about 7 meters away from the water source (i.e. lake, river, hose, etc.); and give the learners 2 smaller buckets;

- ensure that the water source is safe (i.e. not fast flowing, no slippery rocks, etc.) and that learners act responsibly near the water;

- learners may opt to conduct the activity in bare feet, so ensure that the area in which you provide the initiative is free from debris like glass, sharp stones, sticks, etc.
- this is a fair weather activity.... it wouldn't be recommended in the winter months (unless of course you are using an indoor pool or tropical location)!

Metaphorm

- effective leadership takes practice and awareness of many internal and external factors;
- in this initiative, the "drum" represents the ability to provide team leadership to a project. For the most part you will realize the project expectations, but sometimes you will miss some expectations (these misses are represented by the holes).
- "water that is brought to the drum" represents the expectations and potential satisfactions brought by learners to the group. Like energy these expectations and satisfactions build on each other;
- the "water overflowing from the bucket" is your group achieving their success by effectively and efficiently satisfying all expectations and minimizing misses.
- the "buckets represent the physical tools" that the learners use to bring expectations to the project (i.e. vision, past experience, skills, etc.); and
- finally the "members of the group" represent the leadership within the organization.

Debrief

- How do you empowering others to help you?
- What are the benefits of collaboration as opposed to individual leadership?
- How do you manage a group's resources successfully?
- Why do you need to identify the issue?
- Discuss the importance of asking for help and communicating needs continuously throughout issue resolution process.
- How can you apply this to the way that your organization needs to function in order to be effective and efficient?
- What new learning have you realized about issue resolution?

Blindfold Maze

www.teambuildingactivities.com/classic

01:55/04:20 720

BLINDFOLD MAZE
WITH TYLER HAYDEN

Team building is what you do with people, not to people.

- Tyler Hayden

BLINDFOLD MAZE

- Intrapersonal
- **Interpersonal**
- Body/Kinesthetic
- Mathematical/Logical

Quick Description:

A blindfolded team must find their way out of a maze that is a circle. The only solution is asking for help. Once the team member asks for help their problem is solved. Instills the capacity that asking for support from other team members helps to ensure effective and efficient conclusions to issues.

Time it takes:

30 to 40 minutes

Terminal Objective

The session will provide learners with an opportunity to experience the resources that are required for successful issue resolution.

Enabling Objective

The learners will be able to:

- identify the need to ask for help from others;
- discuss the idea of multiple resolutions to issues;
- create an opportunity to aid each other in resolving an issue;
- discuss benefits of helping someone achieve success in issue resolution;
- create a methodology to resolve issues; and
- have fun.

Initiative Task

Blindfold Maze

- it is very important that you set up this activity prior to doing this session so that you can blindfold and walk your learners to its location;

Set Up Considerations:

- this activity needs to be set up on a level a piece of ground that is free of protruding rocks and roots;
- tie a rope from point to point (i.e. tree to tree) so that you end up where you started and there is no opening (see diagram below); and
- clear away any sticks or rocks that are in the activity space.
- blindfold learners in a spot where they cannot see the Blindfold Maze (try to be as close as possible to the maze as the purpose of the initiative is to get them in the maze, not the walk leading up to the maze which has limited educational value for this experience);
- once individuals are blindfolded, ask them to hold each others' hands so that they create a line in which everyone is connected;
- inform them that you will need to take a brief walk that will require them to remain totally silent so that they can hear your instructions on where to walk. Remind them to respect each other and support one another on the walk so that everyone arrives safely and unscathed (that would be 50 cent word);
- safely walk the group to the area where you have set up the Blindfold Maze and position the learners inside the maze enclosure. It looks like this (tree alternative should be a sturdy location i.e. table, door handle, etc.):

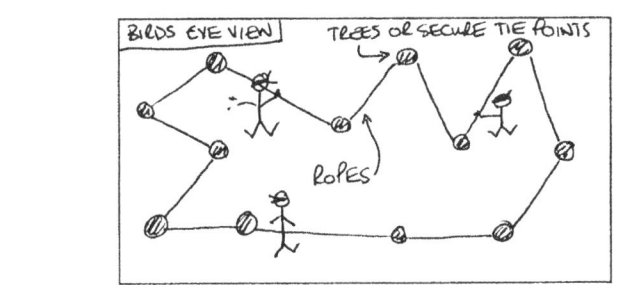

•

- have each learner hold onto the rope (I find it works well if you position them at various points around the maze, this makes it so that they don't run into one another as readily);
- with your learners standing still, explain to them that, "The rope that you are holding represents your time to personal success. Currently, you are all holding a different point within the project. This is because everyone has different skill levels and positions with respect to the project (for example, one person might have an existing template they can use for their part of the project while another does not), so they would naturally start at different points. The time line (or rope) follows a path that will lead to project completion (the exit to the maze). You must successfully complete the project. However, if you need a hand finding the successful completion of the project all you have to do is ask for "help" and someone will support you. You must continue to wear the blindfold as it represents the uncertainty of what comes next in the project because it is hard to anticipate everything that can happen along the way to the realization of the project. Are there any questions?";
- now let the learners go and try and find the way out;
- when someone asks for "help" walk directly over to them, remove their blindfold, motion for them to be quiet, and guide them under the rope;
- have that learner sit off to the side or you can have them help you remove others from the Blindfold Maze when they ask for "help"; and
- do this until everyone is out of the maze.

Debrief
- the focus of this debrief is to look at the idea of resolving issues by getting help from others within an individual's circle of influence. Dialogue should include issues including but not limited to:
- empowering others to help you;
- the benefits of helping others;
- the importance of asking for help;
- following up with people when they help you;
- and managing other team members while they are working on a project.

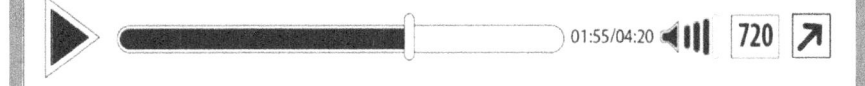

Maze of Frustration

www.teambuildingactivities.com/classic

01:55/04:20   720

MAZE OF FRUSTRATION
WITH TYLER HAYDEN

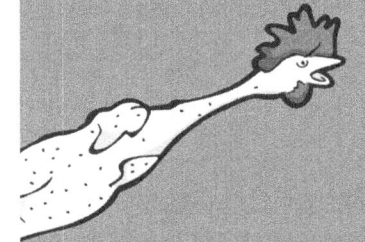

Team building is what you do with people, not to people.

- Tyler Hayden

MAZE OF FRUSTRATION

Naturalistic | **Interpersonal** | **Body/Kinesthetic** | **Mathematical/Logical**

Quick Description:

Group members will attempt to work their way through a maze that has no solution. The facilitator will create an experience that is frustrating and causes the group to break down and experience conflict. This will be done in a controlled environment thereby allowing fruitful discussion around how to resolve issues, even when emotionally charged.

Time it takes:

30 to 60 minutes

Terminal Objective

The learners will experience a spectrum of conflicts and learn to manage them effectively while resolving an issue.

Enabling Objectives

Learners will be able to:

- investigate conflict both individually and collectively;
- resolve an issue;
- construct an issue resolution framework;
- explore success both individually and collectively;
- apply frustration and success to their leadership position;
- plan to manage the emotions of a frustrating task; and
- have fun.

Initiate Task

Maze

- construct a maze on the floor 5 squares across and 8 squares down;
- on a sheet of paper, draw a grid with the same dimensions as the one on the floor;
- now mark several different routes through the maze (mark the different lines with a code to make it easier to keep your place). This is your answer card;
- line up the entire group on one side of the maze and tell them these rules: 1) to succeed everyone must make it through the maze on the same path; 2) if you get buzzed everyone must return to the beginning; 3) you can step forward, backward or side to side, not diagonally and you can't jump; and 4) you have to go one at a time. (If they ask you questions for clarification say nothing else just repeat the rules in order 1, 2, 3 and 4);
- sit down beside the activity and say "go";
- as they step correctly make a bell sound "ding, ding, ding" and when they step on the wrong square make an annoying buzzer sound "ennnnch";
- have the group work their way down a path with some success, then on a square that was previously correct make it wrong and switch to a different path;
- do this several more times until their joy turns to frustration;
- ask the group to give you a personal weather report (i.e. are they sunny? rainy? foggy? or is there a tornado? or perhaps a hurricane?)
- tell them to continue;
- let just a few members out, then change the route yet again (you can even chuckle at their errors) members must start again;
- let people get super mad even pissed off at each other, themselves, and you. Continue to do weather reports; and
- when you are satisfied that the group is as frustrated as you can make 'em stop the activity. (WARNING: This activity can be very charged and if the debrief and process of the event is not handled with care and professionalism you can set your group back. Use with caution.)

The Maze is set up like this:

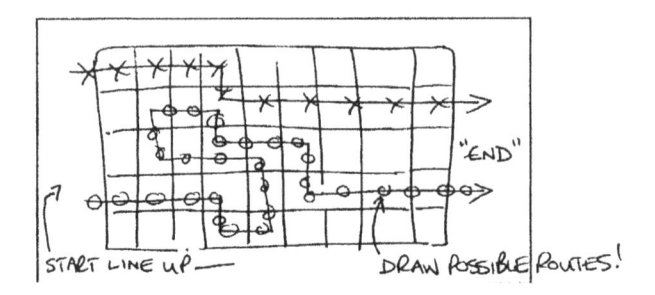

[Hand-drawn diagram of a grid maze with X marks, circles showing a path, labeled "START LINE UP" on the bottom left, "END" on the right, and "DRAW POSSIBLE ROUTES!" on the bottom right]

Debrief

- *let the games begin!*
- *groups will tend to discuss the feelings that they had towards you, each other, themselves - keep it appropriate, professional, and even light - remember it's a training activity. This debrief requires EXPERT skill level - if that is not you, DO NOT ATTEMPT;*

- Ask them to explore what was happening when they got frustrated;
- What were they doing when they were working well together?;
- What caused their personal frustration?;
- How did different people deal with their frustration?;
- How will they deal with frustration with the group as a whole or with individual group members; and
- Why is it important to know how you deal with frustration?
- How does a problem solving framework need to adjust based on changes in the environment/situation?
- Have you ever experienced frustration like this at work? How did you resolve it?
- What happens to issues left unresolved? How does that affect workflow? team?

Team Building Events & Activities for Managers - T.E.A.M. Series

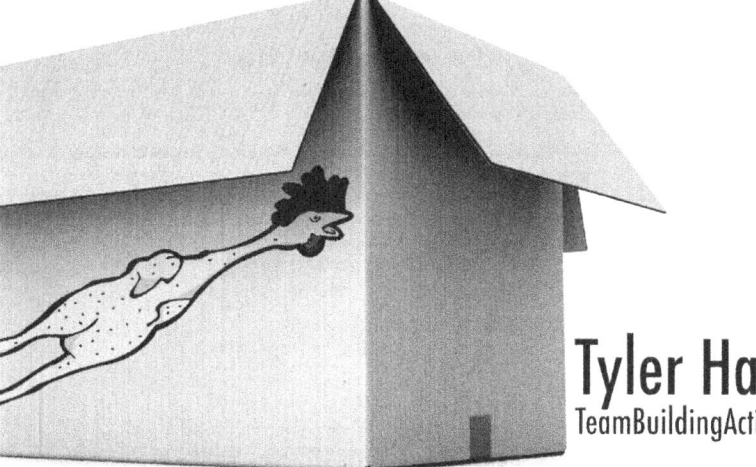

TEAM
TEAM BUILDING ACTIVITIES

Tyler Hayden
TeamBuildingActivities.com

A collection of classic initiative tasks that will help you facilitate experiences that will bring your team together, by taking them outside the box.

BUILD YOUR TEAM'S
TEAM BUILDING SKILLS
WITH CLASSIC INITIATIVES

Warning - Use at Your Own Risk

Improper use of the contents described herein may result in serious injury or loss. The activities should not be attempted without the supervision of a trained and properly qualified leader.

Neither the author, publisher, seller or any distributor of this publication assumes any liability for loss or damage, direct or consequential to the reader or others resulting from the use of the materials contained herein, whether such loss or damages results from errors, omissions, ambiguities or inaccuracies in the materials contained herein or otherwise. No warranties, express or implied, as to the merchantability or as to fitness for any particular use or purpose are intended to arise out of the sale or distribution of this publication and this publication is sold "as is" and "with all faults." The liability of the author, publisher, seller, or any distributor of this publication on account of any such errors, omissions, or ambiguities, shall in any event, be limited to the purchase price of this publication.

Copyright © 2016 by Tyler Hayden Inc.
Livin' Life Large™ is the property of Tyler Hayden Inc.

All rights reserved. No part of this publication may be reproduced, stored in a retrieval system or transmitted in any form or by any means, electronic, mechanical, photocopying, recording, or otherwise, without the prior written permission of the owner.

Made in Canada.

WWW.TEAMBUILDINGACTIVITIES.COM

Team Building Activities

Mammoth Monument

www.teambuildingactivities.com/classic

MAMMOTH MONUMENT
WITH TYLER HAYDEN

Team building is what you do with people, not to people.

- Tyler Hayden

MAMMOTH MONUMENT

Intrapersonal · Visual/Spatial · Verbal/Linguistic · Interpersonal

Quick Description:

Blindfolded member walks through a zone covered with mouse traps and stuffed toys. This member is being lead by only a trusted voice of another team member. All the while other members of the group try to lead them off course and into "danger."

Time it takes:

30 to 60 minutes

Terminal Objective

This session will generate an icon that serves to represent the group.

Enabling Objectives

Learners will be able to:

- experience what it is like to work as a group towards a common goal;
- identify personal attributes that lend themselves effectively to achieving the group goal;
- examine how to communicate within a large group; and
- have fun.

Initiative Task

Mammoth Monument

- begin by talking about how each project team has the opportunity to be individual and quite spectacular, this happens because each member of the team brings different attributes and not team has the same make-up;
- ask individuals within the group to pull out an object they brought with them that represents who they are (i.e. broken clock for someone who's always late, teddy bear for someone who's cuddly, etc.);
- the group must construct a Mammoth Monument to themselves. To do that each individual must partake by first saying their name and saying what the object is and why it is a good representation of a positive quality they possess for the monument (with a large group you need to find some way to run people through the activity at a steady speed)– a sample presentation would be "Hi, my name is Tyler Hayden and this is my favorite work glove because when push comes to shove you can always count on me to get the job done.";
- then the individual affixes the object to the other objects (you should have on hand nails, glue, etc. and a structure for the group to stick the objects to - i.e. a wooden chair, a plywood sheet, a section of tree, a piece of material, etc.); and
- when everyone has placed and introduced their object, the group is to name the structure. Then the monument can be put in a place of honor for all to see...

Debrief

- discuss the content of the activity around such issues as: maintaining individuality, letting everyone be seen, playing an important role in the group, how each person is required to complete the task, how you will function within this large group, how to maximize everyones individual strengths, etc.

20 Questions

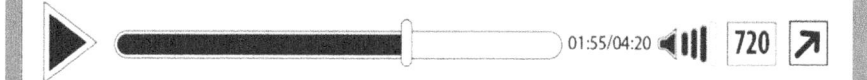

www.teambuildingactivities.com/classic

20 QUESTIONS
WITH TYLER HAYDEN

Team building is what you do with people, not to people.

- Tyler Hayden

20 QUESTIONS

Intrapersonal · **Visual/Spatial** · **Verbal/Linguistic** · **Interpersonal**

Quick Description:

Members answer 20 random questions on a piece of paper. They then consider one question and make a drawing to represent it. Then, each member crumples their paper into a snowball and throws them at each other. After the snowball fight each person collects a snowball and attempts to match the response to the team member.

Time it takes:

20 to 40 minutes

Terminal Objective

Learners will be able to begin to develop relationships with one another.

Enabling Objective

Learners will be able to:

- Learn the name of 5 people in the group;
- prepare to work together as a team;
- share skills and understandings in a safe learning environment;
- work on breaking down interpersonal barriers; and
- have fun.

Initiative Task

Briefing

Take this opportunity to spend some time and introduce yourself... tell them a bit about where you are from and what you like to do (be careful not to make it look like you are stealing the show... but just that you want to introduce yourself). Spend some time also letting the people know a bit about what they can expect from you as a project leader... ask your group if they have any questions... answer them to the best of your ability... then invite them to get involved in the first activity!

Commonalities

- divide into groups of three;
- each small group is to find as many things as they can that they collectively have in common; and
- after 5 minutes each group reports back to the large group.

Cooperative Drawing

- each person, using a different colored pen, creates a squiggly line or scribble (the only rule is no intersecting lines) and passes it to the person on the right;
- this person (on the right) makes a drawing out of it. Setting a theme can help;
- when a squiggle is received it can be rotated in any direction to get an idea what to make out of it. The drawings can be wild and imaginative, they are not judged, they're just for fun; and
- the results usually bring lots of laughter.

20 questions?

- sitting in a group have each learner pull out a piece of paper and a writing utensil;
- next explain to the learners that the following exercise is designed to get you to know yourself a bit better and share a bit about yourself with the group;
- the activity is performed like this: you will read out a question from the list below to the group... they will have 15 seconds to respond to it on their paper... after the 20 questions have been read they will get into pairs and share their answers with each other for 3 minutes each... then the pairs will return to the large group and introduce this person to the group (30 seconds)... And then finally... the snowball fight!
- But before the snowball fight errr... I mean debrief, here are the questions to ask:

1. List 5 words that best describe you.
2. What is the most important thing in your life right now? Why?
3. What do you see yourself doing two years from now?
4. How do you spend your time after work and on weekends?
5. Of all the things that you do in your free time, which do you like the most?
6. What is your favorite TV show? Why?
7. What qualities do you respect and admire in people?
8. How do you think they got the caramel inside the Caramilk bar?
9. What are 3 of your major goals, right now?
10. If you won a million dollars what would you do with it?
11. What is your all time favorite movie?
12. What is the craziest thing you have ever done?
13. Who is your favorite band or musician?
14. Name a role model in your life? Why are they a role model for you?
15. Do you eat Chunky soup with a fork or a spoon, 'cause it is the soup that eats like a meal?
16. Where do you go to relax? Why is this a good place for you to relax?
17. What is your favorite saying or quote?

18. What is your favorite possession?
19. What has been your greatest success in life so far?
20. What is one thing people wouldn't know about you, that would be surprising, that you would like to share?

Snowball Fight

- each member of the group now chooses one of their responses to the above listed 20 questions;
- without showing anyone else, they write out a brief answer to the question and draw a picture that represents the response... so for example if they said their favorite TV show is Drew Carey (which is a good choice!) they might draw a picture of Drew and Mimi...;
- when everyone is finished they crumple up the paper into a paper ball or "snowball";
- then they throw the snowballs at each other just for fun;
- finally everyone picks up a snowball and tries to identify whose it was.
- alternatively you can just throw the 20 question response papers as snowballs and people can read all the answers and see if they can figure out who fits the list :)

Old Fort Henry

www.teambuildingactivities.com/classic

01:55/04:20 | 720

OLD FORT HENRY
WITH TYLER HAYDEN

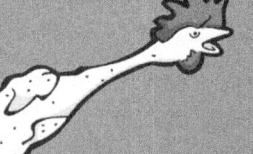

Team building is what you do with people, not to people.

- Tyler Hayden

OLD FORT HENRY

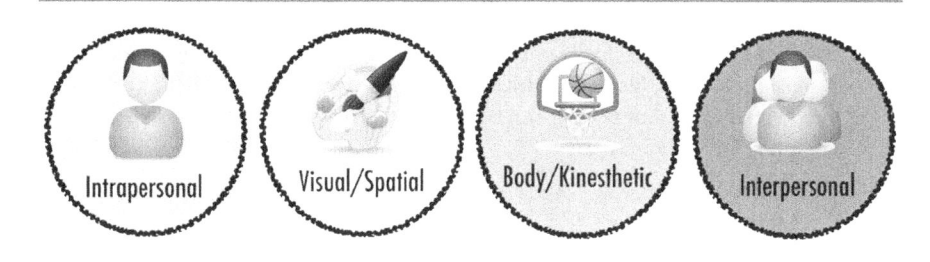

Intrapersonal · **Visual/Spatial** · **Body/Kinesthetic** · **Interpersonal**

Quick Description:

The team will be charged with the task of building a fort that can house all its members using only tape and newspaper. You can increase the challenge by adding features to your "fort" like doors, windows, etc. The event offers an opportunity to talk about different roles that are played within a team. In addition, you metaphor the building/completion of the fort to the project or task of the team.

Time it takes:

30 to 45 minutes

Terminal Objective

Learners will be able to experience a controlled examination of their team skills for competing a project.

Enabling Objective

Learners will be able to:

- identify their own personal role within the team;
- expose themselves to an experience that requires individuals to reverse their roles;
- utilize personal skills to the successful completion of a task; and
- have fun.

Initiative Task

Briefing

Ask your group what the term "teamwork" means. How do the actions and reactions of a leader affect team? Explore some of the positive skills people bring into a team experience (i.e. energizer, summarizer, gate keeper, organizers, etc.). Explore some of the adverse skills that people can bring into a team experience (i.e. blocker, regressor, self confessor, etc.).

Old Fort Henry

- give your group the challenge of building a fort out of the materials in your area (including chairs, desks, etc.) along with a bundle of newspaper and tape;
- tell them that they have 20 minutes to build a structure that houses everyone (including you), that keeps people from touching the ground, and encloses everyone inside;
- now observe the group functioning - look for people who are helping, hindering, supporting, observing, creating, clarifying, etc. Use these observations to help spur dialogue about how groups work together in a project environment.

Debrief

- Make a special note at the beginning of this debrief that it is best not to name names. Instead, identify behaviours and the effects those behaviours had. Explain that every behaviour created the success of the group whether it is perceived as developmental or deconstructive... because the deconstructive often turn into the innovative developmental ideas.

- Who did what?
- How did you feel when someone wasn't adding information?

- Why did someone present a certain behaviour?
- How did it effect group success?
- What things helped make you successful?
- What things hindered your success?
- How could you have performed the task better?
- What was the best part of working with others?
- Could you have done it by yourself in the time allotted?
- Why did someone need to present a certain behaviour within the group?

Made in the USA
Monee, IL
13 November 2019